Robert W. PLASTER School of Business

---

by the FIRST GRADUATE

Stephen R. Plaster

Copyright @ 2018 Stephen R. Plaster
All rights reserved.

ISBN: 978-1986507264

Robert W. Plaster

oil on canvas
by Bill Kufahl
circa 2006

DEDICATION

This book is dedicated to the philosophy
"Can't Never Could."
You never fail until you stop trying.

CONTENTS

Dedication	v
Preface	ix
Foreword by John Ashcroft	xiii
1 The Formative Years	1
2 College and the Search for a Career	11
3 Starting a New Life	19
4 Super Propane	23
5 Bob's Secret Asset	29
6 Bob the Father	33
7 Empire Gas Corporation	53
8 Singleness of Purpose	59
9 The Pargas Offer	67
10 Control Expenses	75
11 Politics	79
12 Empire and "Private" Ownership	83
13 Evergreen Investments	87
14 Foundation and Philanthropy	97
15 Family	101
16 Evergreen Historic Automobiles	105
17 Health	109
Afterword	113
Appendix	115

PREFACE

Robert W. Plaster was my father, mentor, pastor, teacher, and best friend. You may have seen his name on some academic institution and wondered, "Who the heck is this guy?" I hope learning about his humble beginnings and the factors that influenced his life is an inspiration as you question whether your day-to-day travails will add up to the success you desire. The road to success has ups and downs, and only on reflection do we see the steady, upward progressions that make a successful life.

I apologize to all the business associates and partners, employees, family, and friends who were integral to my father's successes and accomplishments and who may not be mentioned. This book is about Robert Plaster, and that governing rule kept me from writing a multi-volume set naming all the incredible people my father embraced, loved, and respected. Leaving them out was more difficult than writing another few volumes—and still too many would be left out. Better to stay focused on the subject at hand.

My father included all his children in his business schedule, and his children and later grandchildren were the first students of the Robert W. Plaster School of Business. Their "curriculum" was based on their interests and talents. In leaving out my sisters and cousins, I made tough decisions. Dad boasted that each of his daughters earned a doctorate and sustained a healthy career: Cheryl Jean became a Professor of Physics at Missouri State University; Tammy Jane a psychologist with her own thriving practice; and Dolly Francine a veterinarian with her own clinic, and later Director of the Robert W. Plaster Foundation. Not only did my sisters spend many hours and weeks in their childhood keeping me in line, but they also enriched my parent's life in ways I may never understand and that Mom, Dad, and I appreciate. Any mistakes are entirely mine.

Past generations read stories about success, courage, and the like—heroes in movies and books were role models. Since the anti-heroes of the 1960s, many generations have had negative role models, so success seems like an old-fashioned ideal. Let's try to make at least this one life real to you.

I worked "for" Dad in many capacities and eventually earned my stripes to work "with" him. Therefore, I claim to be the "first graduate" of the Robert W. Plaster School of Business. My siblings are graduates as well and added significantly to Dad's life and mine, and to his accomplishments and our philanthropy today. We continue to operate the portion of Dad's 500 plus corporations that still exist and several new entities that have come about since his passing.

You will also read why Dad created the Robert W. Plaster Foundation to help institutions of higher education. I hope you won't be subjected to learning too many things you don't really care about.

Dad was a great father and a successful provider. As his "first student," I know he was an intuitive teacher who taught me even when I was not aware of it. With a little luck, I will pass some of those pearls on to you. I hope you enjoy Dad's teachings, wit, and wisdom and wish you the best of happiness, luck, and success in your chosen field.

—Stephen R. Plaster

FOREWORD

The wisdom of United States President "Silent Cal" Coolidge was timelessly expressed when he observed, ". . . Nothing is more common than unsuccessful men with talent." It takes vision, persistence, ambition, and courage to link capacity with great achievement.

In this biography, we witness the convergence of the components of greatness essential to accomplishment. America is not merely unique for the opportunity it fosters, but America is distinguished from many other cultures by items not required—bloodlines, pedigrees, or vaunted credentials.

Ambition if you will, sometimes discredited as self-oriented, has worked its magic for public good and individual greatness again and again throughout our history. Washington in his early twenties was publicly criticized for his "naked ambition." Lincoln, obsessed with being known and remembered was a scant 23 when first a candidate for office. When elected to the State Legislature in 1854, he declared his candidacy for the U.S. Senate a mere 72 hours later.

Focused, properly channeled ambition becomes a bridge to span the gulf between talent and greatness.

The Plaster narrative of this book traces ambition that matures to greatness—great achievement and great generosity. This is not the story of the American dream. It is a history of the American reality. And, a crucial part of Bob Plaster's ambition was to demonstrate the undeniable fact that America is more than a "dream environment"; It is a framework for maturing ambition resulting in generous greatness.

As you read the pages following, you will sense you are reading a constructive blueprint for visioning and achieving greatness.

You will note that Bob learned from others. Reminiscent of Vanderbilt's meetings with Firestone, Ford, and Edison, Bob invited the brightest and best to join him at his beloved Empire Ranch in Laclede County. There, the Biblical principle of iron sharpening iron refined Bob both as a listener-learner and a sharing contributor.

Greatness requires a forward lean—a focus on the future—and a desire to shape the tomorrows in which we live. This consuming awareness led Bob to give and receive counsel from the highest-ranking public policy decision makers equipping them with the capacity to preserve the framework of liberty for generations to come.

Bob knew that shaping the next generation would be the key to the endurance of values that support human dignity and growth. His resulting charity for institutions that train students for beneficial achievement is most commendable. Like Carnegie, whose riches modeled both the path to wealth and its beneficial deployment (Carnegie built over 2,500 libraries), Bob Plaster's charity is designed to foster and enable achievement through self development, responsibility, hard work and growth.

This story of American reality is likely to leave you joining me in gratefully saying that America needs more men of ambition, wisdom, action, and generosity such as Bob Plaster.

By John Ashcroft

U.S. Attorney General Under George W. Bush; Missouri Governor, Senator, and Attorney General

CHAPTER 1

THE FORMATIVE YEARS

Robert Wayne Plaster was born September 3, 1930, in Kansas City, Missouri, the only son of a carpenter and a country girl with considerable skill as a seamstress. This loving partnership was not the ideal economic combination during the Great Depression. Things were always tough and everyone worked to keep food on the table, including younger sister Barbara.

Robert Wayne Plaster, circa 1944

Wayne, as he was known growing up, spent his elementary school summers working at the Elm Springs General Store, a country store owned by his paternal grandparents Tom and Dollie Plaster. His primary responsibility was pumping gasoline from the storage tank into the glass tank above the service point,

A gas pump like the one at the Elm Springs General Store, circa 1940s

which allowed the fuel to be measured as it was sold. This was a lot of work for a little guy and a job he remembered his entire life.

Wayne's responsibilities grew as he did. He found a push mower in the trash and cleaned, rebuilt, lubricated, and sharpened it until it worked like new. Before the gasoline-powered lawnmower (riding or otherwise), edgers, and weed eaters of today, mowing and trimming a yard involved human power—pushing, hand clippers, and a broom. Some neighbors paid as much as fifty cents per yard.

Wayne worked any odd job, from cleaning out basements to digging basements by hand with a pick and shovel; to picking up, hulling, and separating walnuts; to cutting firewood. He literally worked any job that paid.

Wayne discovered there was a demand for live rabbits so he built and placed rabbit traps in the woods. He would leave early

THE FORMATIVE YEARS

Wayne's first lawnmower, 1940s

Elm Springs General Store, Elm Springs Missouri, circa 1935

to check the traps, sell the rabbits when he got to town for something like five cents apiece, and proceed to school.

His next big career move came when the U.S. Government built Camp Crowder, a U.S. Army military base near his hometown of Neosho, Missouri. He learned about their almost constant demand for newspapers. If he took all of the newspapers he could carry—two shoulder bags weighed about 100 pounds—and worked hard to sell every one, he could make as much as two dollars a day. During high school, he worked as a stock boy and janitor for Hunsakkers store, making around seven dollars a week.

Wayne was one of the first students at Neosho High School to attend school half a day so he could work the other half to support the family after his father died. Wayne made good grades, worked hard, and aspired to college.

Plaster Grandparents

Robert Osborne Plaster, Wayne's father, was born to Thomas Jefferson Plaster and Bertha Dollie Dhalluin Plaster (Osborne was Thomas' mother's maiden name). Thomas Jefferson Plaster was a hard-working country boy with English ancestors; Dollie was equally hard-working, a petite French lady who taught herself to play the piano and thought the world of her grandson Wayne.

Bertha Dollie Dhalluin and Thomas Jefferson Plaster, circa 1897

In the early 1900s, store owners extended credit to their customers and expected weekly or monthly payday payments. The Great Depression of the 1920s and 1930s made it tougher to collect the accounts receivable. Faced with customers who depended on them for their most basic of needs, Tom and Dollie extended too much store credit and lost the store and the adjacent family farm when a local bank called their note—for the total indebtedness of $100. Still, these two entrepreneurs raised four sons who became everything from a successful Kansas City doctor to a hobo who "rode the rails" around the country during the Great Depression.

Wayne's Father

Robert Osborne Plaster was a carpenter who could build almost anything, but during the Depression his family often relocated for work. The family seldom owned an automobile, but when they did, they supplemented their income by cutting, hauling, and stacking firewood.

Robert, his wife Elsie, and their two children would pack everything they owned into an early Hupmobile sedan to move to the next job when

Robert O. Plaster about the time of his marriage to Elsie, circa 1929

necessary. They would roll up the linoleum from the kitchen floor and tie it on the fender and take the one and only mattress and tie it to the roof. The drive from Kansas City to Neosho in this car took two days. Had there been hotels, they would not have had the money to stay in one. At the end of the day when they were tired of traveling, they would pull over to the side of the road, remove the mattress from the top of the car, throw it in an appropriate spot alongside the road, and spend the night.

Robert Osborne Plaster died of lung cancer at the age of forty-two before the days when the link between smoking tobacco and cancer had been made public.

Wayne's Mother

Elsie Ladoskie Honeycutt Plaster, the "Can't Never Could" seamstress, circa 1955

Elsie Ladoskie Honeycutt was born and raised near Yellville, Arkansas. As poor as poor could be, Elsie benefited from her strict Church of Christ upbringing and attended church services whenever they were available. Her father died young of consumption, now called tuberculosis, leaving her mother with two small children to raise. After an appropriate period of mourning, her mother remarried a widower named Young, who also had several children. The family was close and hard-working. Elsie made clothes for the entire family from scratch.

A feisty young woman of twenty years, Elsie married the twenty-six-year-old Robert Osborne Plaster on August 3, 1929. Black Thursday on October 24 of that year was less than three months away and would impact their marriage and their generation. The couple moved to Kansas City for carpentry work where both children, Robert Wayne and Barbara Jean, were born. Some years later, they returned to Robert's hometown of Neosho where Robert died. The young widow raised her children while working as the seamstress for the Williams Brothers Clothing Store on the town square of Neosho. She performed all the alterations for the predominantly men's clothing business. Several years after losing her first husband Robert, Elsie remarried. The second marriage was fraught with difficulties and did not last.

In her commitment to work, Elsie was quick to provide instructions or opinions. She made an art of folding and wrapping a package and creating the matching ribbon and bow. She refused to let any package go out less than perfectly wrapped, so one can imagine how meticulous and appreciated her clothing alterations were.

Elsie remained a devout member of the Church of Christ and died peacefully in her sleep at the age of ninety-two. Her strength of conviction had a profound effect on her family and friends.

> *Dad never pressed his Christian beliefs on anyone, but he made sure his kids were raised in the church and had an appropriate Christian education. The family attended church, Sunday school, and followed all the holidays and traditions of our Christian faith. As we planned our own lives, Dad left us free to make our own decisions and to create our own path. Our relationship with God was clear in the way our parents led their lives and managed their business, and I relish the grounding Elsie's strong faith has carried down through the generations. It is impossible to estimate how much our Christian faith has meant to our family.*
>
> —*Stephen*

I never knew Grandma Elsie to have a husband. She had a few boyfriends over the years, and most of them were great people as well, but she never married a third time. I never thought about it because she never complained or whined about being alone and unmarried.

When she was in her eighties she visited my family and made it a point one evening to tell all of us that her second husband had passed away and that she was now free to remarry. Upon questioning her, she responded that in her wedding vows to her second husband she had promised the good Lord that they would be joined in holy matrimony "until death do us part." Her religious belief was strong enough that she refused to remarry for some fifty plus years because that husband was still alive.

I came to admire the strength she showed, not only in that belief, but also in living with that belief. This world would be a better place if more people believed, behaved, and lived with their commitments as she did. —Stephen

Elsie and her son Bob at her last home in Neosho, Missouri, 2005

LESSONS LEARNED

1. Can't Never Could

Elsie's "Can't Never Could" philosophy made her a valuable employee. She knew everyone in town and never met a stranger. As a teen, Wayne would say, "I can't," to which his mother replied, "Can't never could." Wayne took the "Can't Never Could" philosophy to heart. He found that he could achieve almost anything if he wanted it badly enough. Approaching each day, each job, and the world with a "Can't Never Could" attitude drove his success.

Wayne's children, as well as his employees, from line staff to executives, were taught "Can't Never Could: You never fail until you stop trying." If you remember nothing else from reading about Robert W. Plaster, adopt this attitude. It will serve you well.

2. Prioritize

Long after the children were grown, Elsie continued to work and remained self-sufficient. Son Wayne was inspired to work hard to help feed the family.

As Wayne grew and prospered, he kept Elsie in an appropriate automobile, built her a new house, and called every morning on his way to work from wherever he was in the world. He checked on her, told her good morning, and reminded her he loved her. She was, without a doubt, the most influential person in his life. Plaster would claim nothing came before business, but if someone was sick, he was there, at least until he had assessed the problem, the cure, and the danger. Then he delegated caregiving to his wife or his offspring. Family came first, even if he never admitted it.

CHAPTER 2

COLLEGE AND THE SEARCH FOR A CAREER

In high school, Plaster worked hard at odd jobs and a full-time job as a stock boy/janitor/go-for at a grocery store in Neosho for seven dollars a week. By graduation he had saved enough to pay for one semester at Joplin Junior College, now known as Missouri Southern State University. Wayne knew that people who had money knew how to get and to manage their money. Accounting was the logical major.

Robert Wayne Plaster, high school graduation 1948

Before calculators or computers, most math was calculated in your head. Plaster learned and mastered the art of quick, accurate mental mathematics. His talent was an invaluable asset throughout his business career because he never needed to depend on someone else or a machine for calculations.

This ability to calculate different alternatives quickly gave him the upper hand in negotiations. He could look at a spreadsheet and know if it was accurate, which ensured that decisions were based on true not erroneous data.

> *A few years before Dad passed away, we attended a function at his alma mater. A former professor and he caught up on old times; she told Dad that, in all of her years as an accounting professor, he was the only student who ever turned in a final test that was 100 percent correct. This was the first he had heard of it, and he was flattered. —Stephen*

Like many students of the era, Plaster ran out of money and quit college to work. There were no government grants or student loans. He targeted his three semesters to maximize his hard-earned tuition dollars and took primarily accounting classes.

World War II ended in 1945, the Great Depression was winding down, and America was entering a period of great prosperity. Factories were converting from war to civilian use, although metals and materials were in short supply. Used automobiles had been worn out, rebuilt, and worn out again throughout the war years when new automobiles were not even manufactured.

After the war, demand for automobiles was high, and veterans, like the son of the local grocery store owner, received special dispensations to purchase a new automobile. The grocery store owner's son owned a 1937 DeSoto Convertible Coupe, which had very little value due to its age and condition. He tried in vain to sell it.

COLLEGE AND THE SEARCH FOR A CAREER

1938 Desoto Convertible Coupe

One day he approached young Wayne and said, "I don't know anyone in the whole wide world that wants an automobile worse than you do. Here's the title and the keys to my DeSoto. I want $200 for it and you just pay me when you get the money." Wayne accepted the car reluctantly because he was not sure he could afford it, but he paid $2 a week until the entire $200 was repaid. This was Wayne's first, treasured luxury.

Pet Milk

After high school graduation, Plaster was offered a job with the largest employer in Neosho. The Pet Milk Company processed raw milk, creating condensed and homogenized milk and other dairy products. This job paid $12 a week

Wayne Plaster, circa 1948

and was considered the best job in town. Wayne accepted the offer and saved for college.

At the end of the day shift, he disassembled all of the glass piping that had been used to transport the raw milk around the facility. He then cleaned and reassembled it so that it was 100 percent sanitary and ready for the next day. Within a few months, Plaster realized he could probably build this job into a lifetime career, but as lucrative as it might seem, he did not want to spend his life cleaning pipes. He quit and took a decrease in pay to $8 a week to work as an accountant for a local Neosho Dodge/Hudson/Nash car dealership, Robbins Motor Company.

Robbins Motor Company

Jess Robbins was a car guy, a man's man, and a mentor. While working as the accountant, Jess taught Wayne to sell so well that he developed into one of Robbins Motor Company's best salesmen. He sold an automobile to a revenue agent for the Internal Revenue Service, who was so impressed that he encouraged Wayne to take the Civil Service Examination. Each time the agent came through Neosho, he would stop and talk to Wayne about the advantages of a steady government job. After a few years, Plaster took the test and aced it.

LESSONS LEARNED

1. Don't Be Afraid of the Clock

Wayne said the difference between mediocrity and success is an hour a day. He determined that if an hour a day could make you successful, then two or three hours a day would make you very successful, and even more hours would be even better.

Wayne was working when he got up in the morning and he was working when he went to bed at night—if not on the phone then at least planning the next day, what he could do to solve a problem, and what he could do to improve his company and community. When someone would ask what he was thinking about, he would reply immediately, "Making money."

Throughout the normal workday, Plaster would put off a meeting if he knew the participants would be at the office after normal office hours. He could hold that meeting after 5 p.m. His employees were ingrained to understand the difference between mediocrity and success and that the clock was a tool to set and keep appointments. Successful entrepreneurs are not afraid of the clock; it does not dictate their start and stop times.

2. Return Every Phone Call

Salesmen learn fast that they cannot predict who will buy. If anyone goes to the trouble to call, it is about something that concerns them, and it is probably about something that concerns you.

Plaster always returned a call. He returned every call, whether from the janitor from the factory down the street, the dirt farmer from the smallest town in Missouri, or a head of state. If someone called Bob Plaster, he called them back.

3. Make Eye Contact, and Offer a Firm Handshake

Plaster learned to look every person in the eye when he spoke or was spoken to, and to add a firm handshake when he met or saw them. Not crush their hand, but shake it with meaning as he introduced himself. He made sure his children and employees followed this courtesy, one that helped him through every aspect of his life.

If Bob was talking and you looked away, he would stop talking. When you looked up to see why he had stopped talking, he would be looking right at you and would begin talking again. In business he would not work with anyone who would not look him in the eye. Eye contact adds weight to your words. Non-verbal cues add more information than anything you just hear.

4. Working Hard vs. Working Smart

Sweeping a parking lot with a whisk broom would be working hard. Using a leaf blower to clean the same lot in a fraction of the time is working smart. As a boss, Plaster paid fairly and expected his employees to work long and hard. Hard work did not mean just being busy, it meant being productive. Just working "hard" may never add up to your, or more importantly, your employer's goals. Working hard to contribute to your personal success or to the success of your employer—that's working smart.

Early in his professional career, Plaster met with Mr. Piper of Piper Aircraft. The two executives hit it off, and Mr. Piper invited Plaster on a tour of his unionized airplane manufacturing facility. Plaster asked, "How many people work here?" Without missing a beat Mr. Piper replied, "About half."

Many employees, particularly in a factory situation, make it through the day putting in their time, watching the clock, waiting for lunch, and waiting for quitting time. In contrast, the most successful employees work to produce a desired result every minute on the job.

5. Keep Your Personal Life Away from Work

Plaster's wife never called him while he was working. They could talk about family issues when he got home. If there was an emergency, there would be an exception.

Plaster devoted 100 percent of his energy to his job during his workday. His career benefited greatly from this, and his family did not suffer at all. When he went home, he gave his wife and children 100 percent as well.

CHAPTER 3

STARTING A NEW LIFE

While walking across the town square in Neosho, someone made a comment to Wayne. At that moment he realized that no matter what he became or how successful he was, he was always going to be perceived as his father's son, the poorest kid in town. Right then, he decided that if he was ever going to be someone, he had to leave that little town behind. So, in May of 1954, Plaster and his young wife and high school sweetheart, Mary Jean Richards, left Neosho, his mother, and his job as an accountant to work for the Internal Revenue Service (IRS) in Kansas City, Missouri.

Robert Wayne and Mary Jean, Wedding, February 14, 1951

Wayne Becomes Bob

Not only was the IRS a big career move, Wayne made the conscious decision to use his first name now rather than his middle name. He became Bob or Robert.

The IRS allowed Bob to exercise his God-given accounting talent and he did so with a vengeance. By planning his schedule and working his plan, he could complete more audits than most agents. Auditing a wide variety of businesses introduced Bob to the numbers that made those businesses successful.

The Revenue Agent, 1954

One such audit led him to the Super Propane Gas Company in Lebanon, Missouri. After the audit he claimed the IRS "popped him pretty good," which is to say, the audit ended with a hefty new tax bill for Super Propane.

Military Service

The draft is a powerful motivator for many young men, and as the Korean War developed, Plaster knew he would prefer to join the military with rank and in the branch (Air Force, Army, Marines, Navy) that interested him, rather than be drafted at the bottom in an assigned branch. He took the initiative and joined the United States National Guard, enlisting in Neosho at Camp Crowder.

One of the officers had been buying newspapers from Plaster over the years. He took Bob off to the side, presented him with a stack of military textbooks, and said, "Read these. You're going to be a teacher." Plaster said, "I don't know anything about being a teacher." "Yes, you do. Read those books and you'll be fine."

Plaster was soon pressed into service as an instructor for a battalion of anti-aircraft guns and led the only anti-aircraft battalion from Neosho that was not sent into active duty. Someone had to stay and protect the home turf.

> *Dad spoke of the atrocities of war that were inflicted on his friends during WWII and the Korean Conflict. He flew the American flag proudly, a tradition his companies continue to this day.*
>
> *In his later years, Dad drove Mercedes automobiles as well as Cadillacs. At one point, one of our executives purchased a brand-new Japanese automobile, and Dad teased him about driving "Japanese junk." Our executive retorted, "Well, you drive a German car." Dad's response was, "I remember Pearl Harbor."*
> —Stephen

Plaster left active service as a lieutenant November 1, 1955, claiming over the years that his military service taught him more about leadership and discipline than anything he had ever done. He recommended the military to any young person aspiring to a leadership role.

LESSONS LEARNED

1. Build a Boat

Plaster built his first wooden jon boat, a flat-bottomed boat with benches, while working as a revenue agent in Kansas City. On weekends, he guided people floating and fishing the White River south of Neosho. He enjoyed guiding and subsidizing his income.

He built another jon boat in the late 1960s with his growing children, but life got too busy to enjoy guiding. He would say, on occasion, that you can build your own boat but you can't build your own airplane. His logic held that you can generally swim or wade out of any predicament in a boat you built for the river, but if the airplane fails it could be fatal.

2. Spend Every Dollar as if It Were Your Own

Bob taught his children and employees to be frugal with personal as well as corporate money. As son Stephen became more partner than employee and was learning the ropes, he was demonstrating how hard-headed he could be about acquisition opportunities.

Stephen thought the company should make an investment and argued. Bob paused, looked him in the eye and said, "We can continue this discussion tomorrow. Please give this some serious thought and be prepared to tell me if you would make this investment with your personal money as opposed to corporate funds." The next day, Stephen reluctantly admitted that the investment was too risky to make with personal funds. The company did not invest.

CHAPTER 4

SUPER PROPANE

The Super Propane Gas Company in Lebanon, Missouri, was owned by Kenneth Coatney. During his IRS audit, Coatney was impressed by Plaster's winning attitude and confident that Plaster's accounting abilities would improve the company's profits. Coatney courted Bob Plaster for eighteen months in an effort to hire him.

Bob Plaster loved cars, May 1956

In 1957, Plaster, his wife, and one child moved to Lebanon "with a brand-new Mercury automobile and $200 in the bank," Bob would later recount. As General Manager he added accounting controls, halted inventory shortages, stopped product shrinkages, man-

Bob Plaster, Christmas 1958

aged employee hours purchased, and did a host of other things that made the business substantially more profitable.

Propane is a blend of hydrocarbons developed by the Skelly Petroleum Company during World War II. Some veterans returning from war were using their savings to go into the distribution sector of this new propane industry. With low startup costs and few barriers to entry like paperwork, registrations, or regulations, a propane distribution business was easy to start, relatively easy to operate, and profitable.

Shortly after completing his first full year, Plaster and Coatney met to review the finances. When Coatney realized his company had achieved more profit in twelve months than in the preceding ten years combined, he pulled a blank check out of his checkbook, signed it, and told Plaster to go down to the local Cadillac dealer and buy two new identical Cadillacs. Cadillacs were generally considered the ultimate American dream car.

Bob said he might not always be able to afford a Cadillac and he did not want to start driving one until he was sure. Coatney replied, "Get your new Cadillac. Get me a new Cadillac. You will always be able to afford to drive a Cadillac."

To grow, Plaster followed other businessmen of Lebanon as he joined and participated in the good works of the Rotary Club, Shriners, and every other business-related organization. He joined the United Methodist Church, not because it was "better" than the Church of Christ, but because more of the business people of Lebanon attended the Methodist Church. He was active in most social organizations and events in Lebanon.

After a few years, Mr. Coatney's health declined and he decided to sell. Plaster spoke with potential investors nationwide, then arranged the sale to a partnership of Chicago investors.

Plaster continued to manage the growth of Super Propane for the new owners, and after a couple of years the new owners saw an opportunity to cash in with a handsome profit. They instructed Plaster to find another buyer. Plaster met with more potential buyers and the company was sold to Gulf Oil. Plaster received a handsome financial bonus for putting the sale together.

Gulf Oil offered him a position that probably would have been a lucrative career move, but he decided against it. Plaster woke the next morning with a problem that he had never faced—no job, no office, and nothing to do. He began to develop a plan.

A few months later, Plaster himself seized this opportunity. By now he knew how to manage an independent retail propane distribution company successfully, and he decided to work for himself.

LESSONS LEARNED

1. It's Better to Overdress

If you are going to a business function, an interview, or a business meeting, a suit and tie (dark suit, light shirt, dark tie) and well-polished shoes are always appropriate. If no one else is wearing a jacket or a tie, you can remove yours, roll up your sleeves, and become as casual as the next person. When you show up in a t-shirt and shorts and everybody else is wearing a suit and a tie, there is no way to dress up or make the situation better.

2. Tell the Truth

There is no stronger or more valuable attribute in an employee or executive (or spouse for that matter) than credibility. Knowing the true facts can make any problem easier to solve. Many things are better left unsaid. However, your attorney or your doctor impacts your life with their opinions, judgments, and recommendations. Be painfully open with these professionals even if you think it's embarrassing or puts you in a bad light. Bob understood that you are better off when you receive advice based on truth not fiction. Telling your accountant something you cannot prove at audit time won't help you.

Bob put great value in credibility. Working together with others demands that you speak the truth, and are given the truth in return.

3. Net Worth Enhancement

Life taught Bob that the bank does not contain all wealth. Money in the bank is rarely even a good investment, unless you are a banker, since inflation will crush your gains. Money has to grow faster than inflation to let the owner get ahead.

Not all assets create net worth. A car that costs $50,000 and goes down in value day after day, may actually DECREASE your net worth. Do not let the cost of your ego, or keeping up with your neighbor, cause you to overspend on things that do not MAKE you money.

> *There was an elderly couple that lived near our ranch. I felt sorry for them. They lived in a small one-bedroom house heated with wood, had a ten-year-old pickup truck, and a small twenty-year-old tractor. They raised chickens, cows, and pigs. They cut their own hay and raised corn for feed. They grew all of their vegetables. They were always working but had time to stop and speak if we came by. When the husband passed away, the wife moved to town, and we bought their farm. I later found out she had moved into one of about fifty rental properties they owned and had a Net worth of something over $1 million. They just didn't spend any money on ego. —Stephen*

Home ownership properly maintained is net worth not in the bank. Owning assets that have the possibility of appreciating in value such as a piece of vacant real estate, a rental property, an antique car, a work of art, a gun, and many other assets, can increase your net worth substantially. Net worth is the total value of your assets minus your total liabilities. When you borrow money to purchase a company, and through hard work, effort, management skill, or other means you manage to make that company worth more, you increase your net worth. Every investment opportunity must enhance net worth—or it isn't an investment at all. Plaster worked to build his net worth, not his bank account.

4. Listen to Experience

Bob's closest friends were older and he could learn more

from them. He listened. By his seventies, he was that older man doing the teaching. He often quoted his older friends. Learn early to respect the ideas of your elders. They may not have an education like you do, but they have lived through many years and experiences that you have not.

5. Pick Your Time, Place, and Weapons

Bob used to say, "If you're going to be in a fight, do everything you can to pick the time, the place, and the weapons." Consideration, planning, and forethought went into his negotiations. He picked a time and place when his counterparts would be comfortable, and he had some thoughts in his armada of weapons.

On the other hand, for an already adversarial negotiation, Plaster might pick a time inconvenient for the other guy, a place they are outclassed or uncomfortable, and arm himself with facts that could throw them off-center or catch them off-guard. Confrontations go better when you control the time, place, and weapons.

> *For whatever reason, the IRS audited every Empire Gas Corporation tax return, every year for thirty years. At first, the auditors were provided with executive chairs, an office, access to secretarial services, refreshments, and other amenities. An audit might take several weeks. After a few years, the company changed tact and provided an "audit room" of about seven feet square with a tile floor, no windows, one light bulb, and two "desks." These desks were just Formica shelves on opposing walls with straight back folding chairs and one outside telephone line. Audits from this space were completed in a few days. I like to think this is another example of Plaster choosing time, place, and weapons. —Stephen*

CHAPTER 5

BOB'S SECRET ASSET

Mary Jean Richards' father, Walter "Tex" Richards, retired as a lineman for the Empire District Electric Company in Neosho, Missouri. Bob and Jean, as she was known most of her adult life, were high school sweethearts and maintained a realistic and successful pact. He would earn the living for the family; she would raise the family. Every evening Jean would prepare dinner, feed the four children—Cheryl Jean, Stephen Robert, Tammy Jane, and Dolly Francine—and put them to bed by herself if Bob was not home yet. Bob tried to get home before the kids' bedtime, but Jean was always there to

Left: Sweethearts, circa 1948

Right: Bob Plaster, Jean Richards, and the 1937 Desoto

Bob and Jean Plaster were married for more than 50 years.

manage the household and take care of the children. She would keep his dinner hot in the oven until 10 p.m., when she put it away and went to bed.

Jean was active in the church, her bridge club, and always had a smile for everyone. She signed her name "Mrs. Robert W. Plaster" so the local community knew the Plaster businesses were supporting them. They were married in an era when women were not credited with separate business success, but one of Bob's wisest decisions was his early and lifelong partnership with Jean, whose supportive contribution to his successes were innumerable, unmeasurable, and unwavering.

Many people wondered if Bob Plaster liked them; no one wondered if Bob Plaster loved them. The children may have balked when they were being fussed at, but they knew love. Dad would go out of his way to help those he loved and would advise his family to love with all your heart.

When the subject of marriage came up, Dad suggested adolescents wait until they were thirty years old. To young adults, he would say, "Wait until you are certain. You will not contemplate divorce so readily."

A two-year marriage right out of high school or college may not cost much money, but the emotional toll is immense. After one has assets or breaks up a ten-year marriage, the financial costs could be exponentially more.

Dad recommended prenuptial agreements to negotiate and determine the terms of the divorce settlement before marriage, just like all his partnership contracts had careful "out" clauses. Prenups have to be written carefully to be legal and binding and can be ultimately beneficial to both parties.

Children make a huge difference, and the cost on their lives is immense and irreversible. Children are the lifetime wild card—custody and how one pays for your offspring cannot be predetermined by a prenup. Plaster told his family to put off having children until they were certain the marriage would last. Having a child to try to save a marriage seldom works. —Stephen

Bob and Jean raised four children with totally distinct interests and ambitions, yet each maintains a residence on the ranch. And every Sunday multi-generations of Plasters enjoy family dinner.

Son Stephen wrote this to be hung in that house:

Mary Jean Plaster, 1931–2009

Some called her "Mom" or "Mother"
Some called her only "Jean"
Some called her "Mrs. Plaster,"
but her name was Mary Jean.

Some called her "Grandma Jeano"
and she liked that a lot!
She kept the house and hauled the kids,
her kitchen always hot!

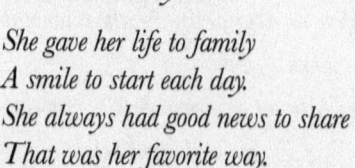

She gave her life to family
A smile to start each day.
She always had good news to share
That was her favorite way.

She made this house a "home" for all;
She kept it filled with love!
She raised, and taught, and loved "her kids"
That's what she thought most of!

Her life was for her family;
that was her only job.
She took care of "the little stuff,"
and loved her husband Bob.

She'll always be remembered ...
and always with a smile.
Her love still seems to fill this house ...
Enjoy it for a while!

—Stephen Plaster, 2009

CHAPTER 6

BOB THE FATHER

Plaster and his children: Cheryl Jean holding Dolly Francine, Stephen Robert, and Tammy Jane, circa 1967

Bob was a tough taskmaster. He expected his children to work hard in school and make good grades; build their own careers; and to be honest, caring, and God-fearing citizens in their own right.

Empire Ranch

In the late 1960s, Bob Plaster needed a place to entertain out-of-town guests and raise his family. He chose a rural area about ten miles outside of Lebanon, Missouri, he called Empire Ranch. With the assistance of architect Bob Evans, who studied with the famous and innovative architect Frank Lloyd Wright, the Plaster Homestead was created.

The first farm was a small one, and he began building a

**Plaster and his children
Cheryl and Steve, circa 1962**

house there. Over the years, he tried to buy any farm that joined his. It was a working farm with cows and sometimes horses. It was soon up to 3,500 acres and making a little money. Bob and son Stephen spent a lot of weekends working, maintaining, upgrading, and planning. This was probably Plaster's only hobby. All the children lived and played on Empire Ranch. Some of the children had jobs working on the for-profit farm, so they never played "team" sports like baseball, basketball, or football. Hefting hay bales and working cattle was more likely.

The farm kept the family close to home. Bob would be called a workaholic today, but most summer weekends were spent on Lake of the Ozarks with or without business guests, who were treated as part of the family.

Family Vacations

Bob did not believe in frequent vacations. But on family vacation, breakfast and lunch were wide open, and the "new food rule" was in force at dinner. Everyone was expected to try some sort of food that we had never tried before.

In 1966, the family rode the Kansas City Flyer from Kansas City to Disneyland in Los Angeles. In 1971, they flew to Disney World in Florida. About 1974, Bob converted a brand-new Cadillac to run on propane. One of his pilots drove the car to Colorado while the family flew out. They used the car in the mountains and parks for a few days, then drove home. Shortly after the propane fill-ups on the Colorado road trip, the Empire Gas Corporation acquired several propane companies in Colorado.

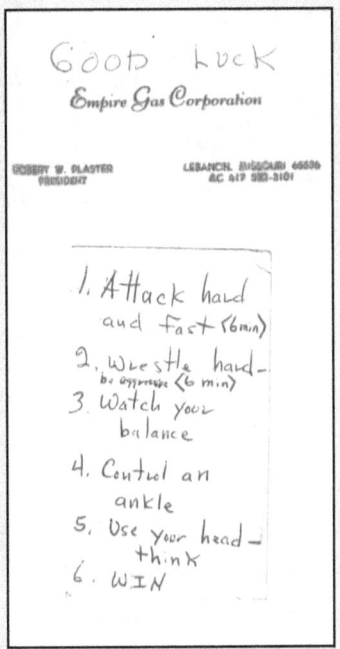

Growing up on the ranch, our nearest neighbor was two miles away. I never really learned much about team sports. But I spent most summers wrestling cows, fence posts, and hay bales, so I joined the high school wrestling team. The most valuable lesson from wrestling is that you can win and your team still lose, or you could lose and the team still win. That is life.

Wrestling was important to me, so Dad went out of his way to attend and film all the matches he could. He might show up just before my time to compete, often talking business with an associate along for the ride, but I rode home with Dad. We never failed to discuss the match. At the time, I did not appreciate what great lengths he must have gone to to punch those holes in his busy schedule to be there for me.

I don't remember resenting the time he was working as too many children do. Sunday afternoons we would watch the Super 8 film match footage he had taken and discuss and critique my performance to ensure I improved.

At one tournament where Dad could not communicate with me directly, he had a note delivered to me on his business card. —Stephen

The Plaster hunting lodge, twelve bedrooms and a large great room, was built in the early 1970s.

Refuge

Eventually, the time required to manage the farm in concert with wildlife habitats was not worth the revenues generated. Around 1976, the entire farm became a wildlife refuge so the wild deer, quail, and turkey could thrive for the enjoyment, hunting, and sightseeing of guests from all over the country. Empire Ranch was probably as close as Bob came to a hobby and something he enjoyed.

In the early 1980s, ten days before the opening day of deer season, Bob Plaster called his son Stephen and said, "I've screwed up and invited too many people to the deer hunt." Stephen replied that some guests could stay at his father's house or his. Bob's "Can't Never Could" attitude would not accept a half-solution, as he replied, "That will not do—let's just double the number of bedrooms to twelve at the lodge."

Gene Sellers, a local contractor, was a dear family friend renowned for his fast, efficient, and cheap construction methods (not to mention his homemade wine!). Nine days before opening day, Bob, Gene Sellers and Stephen met in Bob's office at 8 a.m. Gene opened his first bottle of Baileys Irish Cream as the construction price was negotiated. By 9 a.m., Gene and Stephen were at the hunting lodge as Gene opened his second bottle of Baileys. They drew up a rudimentary set of plans for the addition on a brown paper grocery bag scrounged from the kitchen. Gene created a materials list on a second grocery bag. At 8 a.m. eight days before deer season started, tractor trailers, delivery trucks, and contractors lined up on the one-and-a-half-mile road from the highway to the lodge. By the evening before opening day, the addition was finished, furnished, decorated, equipped with linens, and occupied. Gene walked away with a brand-new Cadillac as his fee.

> *He's known as "Bob" to many,*
> *called "Robert" by a few.*
> *He's "Bobby" to his old friends,*
> *"Mr. Plaster" to his new.*
>
> *Known as "Dead-eye" when he's hunting,*
> *"Big Bad Bob" when dressed in black.*
> *And he may never know what else*
> *he's called behind his back.*
>
> *But no matter what they call him,*
> *through all the good or bad,*
> *I'm proud to say I'm one of few*
> *who call him simply, "Dad."*
> *Merry Christmas Dad*
>   *—Stephen, Circa 1979*

BOB THE FATHER

Bob enjoying time on Empire Ranch

Thousands of stories can be told about driving around the ranch, entertaining through hunts, family time, fighting the elements, and getting stuck. There were picnics and outings large and small, and they created many memories for everyone.

Today, the ranch is 12,000 acres across more than 100 farms that have been allowed to revert to a more natural state. The Missouri Conservation Department will confirm the best deer and turkey hunting in the State of Missouri is on the ranch. Thousands of CEOs, corporate presidents, governors, senators, and all manner of other officials and politicians—plus friends and interesting people from all over the planet, arrive often. The lodge runs entirely at Plaster family expense and by invitation-only. Good times abound and have spring-boarded many fruitful business relationships.

In the mid 1980's, the minister from the local Methodist church (of which I was a member) started making a big push to get me to attend church on Sunday mornings. At that time, I traveled Monday through Thursday most weeks, and the weekends were my only time for relaxation and doing personal chores around the house. Our minister got downright beligerant in pushing me to attend Sunday services. I invited him to hunt deer with us at the Ranch. On that morning, I took him to my favorite "spot." As he was soaking up the majestic view, sights, smells, and sounds of nature, I pointed out to him that when I want to be close to the Lord, I go to the woods. I asked, "How can you get closer to God, in a building full of people, than you are right here?" He was always a friend thereafter, but he never again pestered me about my Sunday attendance. —Stephen

LESSONS LEARNED

1. Avoid a Fight at All Costs

Bob's advice to his children was, "Avoid a fight if you can, as long as you can. Get away if you can. But when you come to that point in time when you cannot get away and you cannot put it off, take the first punch, make it count, and win the fight."

In grade school, a bully who had flunked a few times and was a head taller than his class was causing trouble. Stephen followed this advice to the letter, and the grade school bully is a friend to this day. The advice works in business with competitors, co-workers, and employees. Instead of a fight, the competition is the motivation to produce a better product so the customer is the ultimate winner.

2. Use Proper English

Bob used proper English in business, never cursed, and was often silent. On the ranch or with farm hands, he was casual and so was his language. Raised in a small Midwestern community, his children are bilingual—they can speak English—or American—and they know when to switch.

Executives need an exceptionally good grasp of the English language, including a good vocabulary and a wide knowledge of fields of study and businesses. That one-time-only first impression is determined by what you say and how you say it. Any ambitious young person with goals in the business world must prioritize his English classes and resist the bad habits our American slang presents. We are an informal nation and so is this book, but formality and precise language in business are critical.

Your lawyer and your banker will agree.

Before computers, Bob dictated his outgoing letters, a secretary typed them, and then he proofread and personally signed every letter. This gave him another opportunity to think about what he had said and to change it if necessary. Regardless of whether he was signing "Bob," "Robert Plaster," or "Dad," you knew a Plaster letter was not a form letter drawn up by an underling.

Changing any document is expensive and time-consuming, but the care Plaster took was important to the professionalism of his company and it was considered with the weightiness it deserved. Mass produced, auto-penned letters are more easily dismissed, and many a hastily typed and sent email or electronic communication is regretted.

> *Generally, the best advice in business is, "Say it and forget it, write it and regret it." Sensitive subjects are usually handled better with a phone call or face to face.*

3. Knowledge Is Power

German philosopher Friedrich Nietzsche said, "That which does not kill us, makes us stronger." Bob taught his children while working on the farm, let them sit in on meetings, and inspired them to continue to learn about our world every day. He knew that bettering yourself as a person made you a better executive.

A typical lesson was, "If you are going to enter a golf tournament, wouldn't you practice or get a golf pro to teach you? Unrelated skills can help you in golf—good distance vision and strength endurance training. In business, don't ever be afraid to learn or try something new. Knowledge is power."

4. Know Good Table Manners

The elementary school Plaster children had age-appropriate fun and went to dinner at "fancy" places. How to hold a fork, which fork to use, when to put your napkin in your lap, which glass to use, and all manner of socializing rules were taught.

Sooner or later all of us dine with people important to our present or future—employers, future in-laws, even neighbors. Businesses today often take their potential employees to lunch before they hire or they provide a required course in table manners for new executives–it is that important. Employers are not just reviewing your brilliant résumé or want to use their expense account up—lunch is part of the interview.

European table manners are different. When dining in Europe it is very common to see someone holding their fork in their left hand, their knife in their right, cutting a bite and then eat holding their fork like a screwdriver handle. What is appropriate in Europe may be seen as ignorance in the States.

Many older American executives will just assume that a young American doesn't have table manners if he is eating like a European. Follow European table manners in Europe with Europeans if you like, but if you are an American in America, American table manners will smooth your way to success.

5. Focus on the Light

Everyone experiences dark situations where everything feels wrong, nothing feels right. Bob would tell his children to search in and around that darkness until you find a speck of light, then focus on that speck. Inevitably there will be a way to get to the light and escape all the darkness. The power of positive thinking in "Can't Never Could" works.

6. Vote

In the late 1960s, Bob felt a local referendum should pass and his children heard him encourage everyone to vote in favor of it. In a business meeting election night, Bob learned that his partner and friend Rex Shaddox had not voted. The referendum failed to pass by one vote. Dad never let Rex live that mistake down, and the children learned to pull the lever in an informed vote in every election.

The United States of America has been the most prosperous, free, and greatest country in the world for hundreds of years. The entire political system and thus how this country runs can change with a vote—nothing is as fundamental and as important. If you don't vote, you can't complain!

7. Teach Your Children to Swim

Bob could swim, but it wasn't pretty. That didn't stop him from boating or fishing, but he steered clear of ocean cruises and even overseas flights. He made sure his children knew how to swim and that they were never intimidated by the water.

8. Do Nothing to Help You Fail

Bob told his children, "I will do anything to help you succeed, but nothing to help you fail." Sometimes his children resented his inaction, but if Bob thought it was wrong, trivial, or unimportant, he would not help. If he could help them succeed, he usually helped even before he was asked.

Like many parents, his heart broke when he was forced into "tough love" situations. When your daughter wants to run off with the wrong guy or your son wants the degree of independence he is not ready for, parents should say no. Today's "no" is preparation for future success, but harder to say than it sounds. The most likely place an otherwise successful person fails is in that blind and unconditional part of love held for your children. Care enough to ask where they are going. Care enough to keep them home if they don't have good answers. No good can come from "hanging out." Care enough to say "NO."

9. You Cannot Change a Person's Basic Nature

Making a positive change in someone else's basic nature is hard and usually unsuccessful. Bob taught his children that a good person will tend to remain a good person and vice versa. You can paint it, you can wax it up and make it nice and shiny, but a Ford is not a Cadillac.

Mentoring has its limits. "Management" can make an employee better at a specific task or goal. No amount of effort will change another person's underlying true nature—only a change from within can accomplish that.

10. Know the Difference Between Working Dirt and Dirty Dirt

Plaster taught his children and employees that a salesman getting in and out of the vehicle in all kinds of weather and in all kinds of conditions gets a floor dirty. That is "working dirt." Clean it up at least weekly, but work. Your personal and vehicle appearance are your best sales tool.

However, "dirty dirt" on the floorboard of the car for weeks accumulates water, water causes rust, and first thing you know your vehicle looks terrible and your car smells. Working dirt shows that you work. Dirty dirt shows that you are not paying attention to your appearance, or you are just lazy.

Bob would say the two cheapest things on the planet are soap and paint. Keeping things clean and looking good does more to help your self-image and your first impressions than any other change—in your automobile, your place of business, your home, or your person. The least expensive investment in what is important to you is found in simple, clean maintenance.

> *All too often Dad would talk to me about my job performance. My response generally was, "But I outperformed everyone." His response was, "You proved yourself the best of the worst." Dad was reminding me that a comparison to others was never the yardstick of a man ... did you do your personal best?*
>
> *Everyone is different. Dad would advise that to be successful in life, find out what you do really well that you like to do, then figure out how to do a lot of it.*
>
> —*Stephen*

The Plaster family on the occasion of Grandma Elsie's 80th birthday party.

48 ROBERT W. PLASTER SCHOOL OF BUSINESS

49

50 ROBERT W. PLASTER SCHOOL OF BUSINESS

For years, these four pictures hung on Robert Plasters office wall. When people asked him why he worked so hard, he would merely point at them.

CHAPTER 7

EMPIRE GAS CORPORATION

Bob Plaster knew that the accounting controls and processes that had made Super Propane Gas successful would benefit other independent propane dealers. He had sold the company twice and used his knowledge and connections to find venture capital, so he did not fear managing his own company.

On July 3, 1963, he founded the Empire Gas Corporation, named after a relatively obscure television series about a wealthy entrepreneur who flew around the country in his new Learjet performing good deeds. The office was a rented closet

Empire Gas Corp Headquarters Groundbreaking, *Lebanon Daily Record*, December 2, 1963

"Fueled by LP Gas on His Rocky Road to Success," *St. Louis Post-Dispatch*, July 14, 1969

Empire Gas Corporation headquarters

in the Lebanon, Missouri, Greyhound Bus Station with a desk, a chair, and a telephone.

Plaster's $25,000 contribution was soon joined by financial investments from Chicago entrepreneurs such as Bacon, Whipple & Company. A University of Chicago representative handed him a check for $3 million and said, "Go build us a gas company." Decades later, representatives of the University of Chicago would say Empire Gas Corporation was the best single investment they ever made.

The first independent propane dealer Empire purchased was Webb Butane in Cassville, Missouri. Empire recognized the goodwill of these companies—that intangible value of the reputation of a local company founded by a local veteran and the many jobs created in that community. Therefore, Empire changed the names of any acquisition slowly, although the company colors were changed immediately to green and white, "the color of money," as Plaster often said.

Rex Shaddox

Rex was an independent propane dealer in Springfield, Missouri. His years of operational experience made him a very attractive partner candidate for Plaster. Empire acquired that company and Shaddox joined Plaster in founding the new company.

Bob did what he did best—numbers. Rex managed people, and he was a genius with them. Before the age when employers nursed the growth and self-esteem of each employee, Rex provided every executive with a neat, two-sided display for their desk. Plaster and Shaddox grew Empire into the largest retail propane distributor in Missouri, and

Rex Shaddox, Vice President and Co-founder, *Wall Street Journal,* circa 1965

kept growing. Unfortunately, Rex passed away from a smoking-related heart attack early in 1969.

 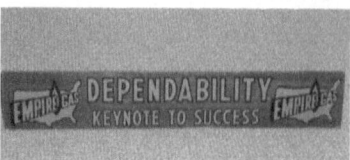

Rex Shaddox gave each executive a desk display, early 1960s

 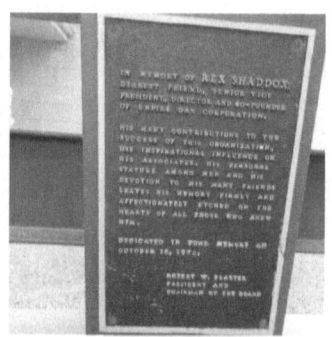

Monument erected in honor of Rex Shaddox, Empire Gas Corporation Headquarters, 1970

When Bob was trying to entice Rex Shaddox to join him in the new propane company, they met and worked numbers and projections on the paper napkins at a restaurant or cocktail lounge. On one such napkin, Plaster showed Rex that they could buy companies based on the seller's cash flow, put in substantial accounting controls, gain economies of scale, produce operating synergies, streamline expenses, and profit more than the individual companies. Rex joined forces with Plaster based on that napkin. Often Rex became disheartened during growing pains, so he would call Bob to ask, "Hey, would you show me that napkin trick one more time?"

Above: Rex Shaddox, Ray Dorr, and Bob Plaster with the first two new Piper Aircraft, *Lebanon Daily Record*, September 17, 1964

Center: Plaster and Shaddox with new Cessna 411, *Lebanon Daily Record*, December 26, 1966

Below: Bob Plaster and Martin Dryden, Jr., with Empire's first jet, Lebanon first jet, *Lebanon Daily Record*, November 11, 1980

The Flying Efficiency

After driving back and forth to Chicago, a seven-hour drive today and much longer then, Bob and Rex took flying lessons. Bob would get the plane up to altitude, set the autopilot, and then read, which was not safe or legal. He decided to hire a corporate pilot but maintained his pilot's license all his life. Both men were qualified to fly every airplane they owned.

Operating a multi-state business from a small town in Missouri made for tough travel connections. Plaster NEVER could have accomplished what he did without using private airplanes. Having a good safe airport brought literally millions of dollars into that little town. Airplanes are expensive to operate and can only be justified by the time they can save, and of course by what can be accomplished in the time saved.

The Non-Smoking Edict

Plaster lost his father to smoking and his Co-Founder, Vice President, and best friend, Rex, succumbed in 1969. That year Empire Gas Corporation made national news when it proclaimed the corporate headquarters to be an entirely non-smoking building. Bob remained an ardent non-smoker and declared every building he ever occupied or owned to be non-smoking.

Empire Gas Corporation's commitment as the first non-smoking headquarters, circa 1970

CHAPTER 8

SINGLENESS OF PURPOSE

Successful executives tend to develop a belief they are capable of managing many types of businesses with equal ability. All too often this over-confidence proves to be wrong as they begin new ventures or add personal investments that fail. One of Plaster's senior executives opened a new restaurant, thinking it would be fun and assuming that his management skills would transfer. The new venture was doomed almost from the start as decisions were made without experience to guide him. The restaurant soon failed.

Early in his career, Plaster developed what he came to call "a singleness of purpose." He dropped out of all his local charitable and social activities and dedicated 100 percent of his productive energy to building Empire Gas Corporation. When aspiring entrepreneurs asked what he attributed his many successes to, "singleness of purpose" was his first and last response. He believed providing customers with excellent service for their propane needs was best, so he focused on growing a healthy company that delivered propane and absolutely nothing else. This singleness of purpose was key to Empire's rapid growth and success.

Plaster led Empire to years of substantial growth and revenue improvements. Only seven years into business, Empire had grown to more than 120 locations in seventeen States.

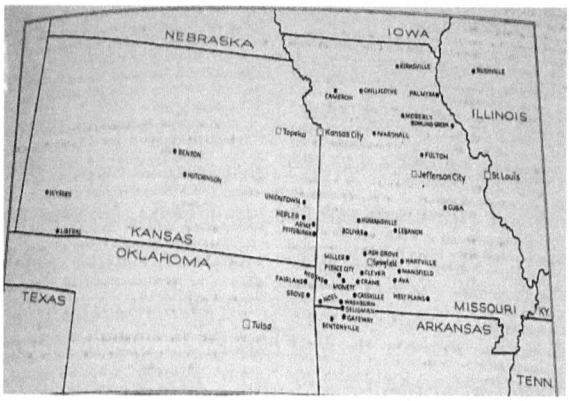

Two-year-old Empire Gas' sixty-eight retail distribution facilities in five States, *Butane-Propane News*, February 1965

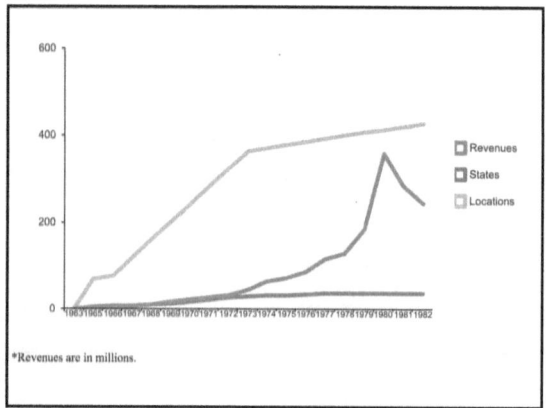

Plaster orchestrated phenomenal growth for Empire, 1963-1982

Management team of Empire Gas Corp. annual report, 1977

Empire Goes Public

Empire's upside looked limitless. The logical thing to do was to consider the big step to public ownership. On January 25, 1971, Plaster took Empire Gas Corporation public on the New York Stock Exchange. Public ownership provided an entirely new pool of investment dollars, and valuable exposure. Both promoted faster and more reliable growth.

Most employees could now own stock in the company and Empire rewarded its executives with stock options. By making their respective areas of responsibility work better and grow, they increased the value of their stock and of Empire as a whole. Most executives came from the same hard-working roots as Plaster so these were dreams made real for many families. Although profit-sharing is common and encouraged in some of the best-run corporations today, Empire was an innovator in the 1960s, especially in propane.

Moreover, Empire tried hard to keep the best and the

brightest employees from every acquisition, which added to their goodwill and kept community customers reassured. The executive talent and buy-in program for stock strengthened the loyalty employees and customers had for Empire Gas Corporation at every turn. The stock split several times and the company continued to prosper.

Plaster (center) at the New York Stock Exchange, opening day January 27, 1971, *Lebanon Daily Record*

LESSONS LEARNED

1. Never Loan Money to a Friend

Plaster always said that "If you loan money to a friend, you will probably lose a friend (and the money)." As Bob became more successful, friends approached him needing money. He sometimes gave it to them but rarely loaned it to them. Bob would say he appreciated them as a friend, and if they didn't pay the money back he would still be their friend because it was a gift. These gifts were almost always repaid, often with interest and often with life-long friendship.

2. Maintain Your Credibility

Bob considered credibility one of the most important, if not the most important, attribute in an associate, employee, executive, or friend. His personal credibility was beyond reproach. If he told you something, you could bet your bottom dollar it was correct. If he promised to do something, he did it. He expected his family and employees to say what they meant and mean what they said, and to honor their word even if it hurt.

3. Avoid Personal Guarantees

Banks lend businesses money because normal businesses borrow money to survive and grow. A good business will be able to service that debt, but the managers cannot control every change in the economy, interest rate, regulation, the weather, or the variety of other factors. Growing up during the Great Depression, Bob saw too many personal guarantees that put otherwise financially secure families and businesses into financial trouble. America's corporate laws are created to draw a line between business and family for just that reason.

Bob never made a personal guarantee for a loan. Empire and later his other companies walked away from banks that required a personal guarantee. If the transaction was sound, the executives found a bank willing to assume the risk with a corporate or entity guarantee. If a deal is not solid enough to support its own debt, an investor should probably avoid the deal anyway.

4. Use Lombardi Time

Vincent Lombardi never had a losing season as a head coach in the National Football League (NFL) and led the Green Bay Packers to five championship titles in seven years. Not coincidentally, he was a great motivator. Showing up "on time" for practice was 15 minutes late. His athletes arrived 15 minutes before "on time" to dress and prepare to be "on time." Bob taught his family and his employees about "Lombardi time" and to manage their time well, and one of those edicts was be prepared and on time.

5. Always Listen ... First

Listening first helps you know exactly what is on the other person's mind. Plaster encouraged other people to talk so he could learn. He encouraged his children and his executives to develop a rebuttal or a response to the other person's opening discussion before speaking. Time and time again the other party's starting point proved to be better than where he would have begun.

In the early 1970s, Empire Gas Corporation became the owner of a surplus Buick Century that was included in an acquisition. The company had no need for the car, and Bob researched the value.

One day an executive asked for a few minutes of Plaster's time, walked into his office, and said, "Bob, I want to buy the little Buick Century, and I will not pay a dime more than $2,500." Plaster immediately responded with, "I want to sell the Buick, and I will not take a dime more than $2,000 for it." Always listen ... first.

6. Keep Many Deals Working

When you are trying to do deals, sales, or find opportunities, it is easy to spend all of your time on that one big deal—the one most likely to close, or the one with the biggest payday in friends, money, or prestige. Empire and Evergreen Investments kept many deals in the pipeline with the overriding goal to add to the bottom line. Plaster would say, "If you keep a lot of balls in the air, one of them is bound to fall sooner or later."

Normally, Bob tried to complete several small deals. If a small deal fails, the company still had all of the other deals working. If the one big deal fails, it may take time to put anything else in motion, and that fact is as true in sales as it is in the business of acquisitions.

CHAPTER 9

THE PARGAS OFFER

The first step to any successful acquisition is a detailed evaluation of all available data. Even in the 1970s, many investors left this process up to merger and acquisition banks and spent a lot of money for the reassurances that the banks knew what they were doing. Plaster and his acquisition team performed all their evaluations in-house.

Based on this internal number crunching, Plaster determined that the total value of the publicly traded stock (called total capitalization value) for their direct competitor Pargas, Inc., was substantially less than what the company was really worth. Pargas was roughly the same size as Empire, but operated in different markets. The synergies of merging two direct competitors—moving the headquarters to Missouri and trimming the fat in the Pargas overhead budget—would have added even more value for the combined entity. The merged company could enjoy the revenues of both companies with the overhead of only one. Empire tried to acquire Pargas on friendly terms, but management would not talk about selling.

Early in 1976, Plaster began using Empire's surplus cash

flow to acquire Pargas stock. The Securities Exchange Commission (SEC) is the government agency that regulates the ownership and stock practices of corporations. After a certain percentage determined by law, any purchase of more stock requires SEC approval.

When Empire had purchased enough shares for SEC permission to be required, Plaster filed, received permission from the SEC, and arranged for bank financing for a leveraged buyout of roughly 60 percent of the outstanding Pargas, Inc., stock. Empire made the appropriate announcement of a "tender offer" for 2 million of the then-outstanding shares, roughly 60 percent of the total.

A tender offer is not a sweet and tender moment with your lover. This is a public, open invitation to current stockholders to purchase their shares at a specific price, date, and time, commonly called "an unfriendly tender." The potential purchaser adds a premium over the current market price, so the stockholder has a cash incentive to sell their shares to the takeover company.

Pargas management was livid. When Pargas realized that the stock-holding public would profit nicely and would undoubtedly sell their shares at the "tender offer" price, management changed their attitude and began to negotiate instead of stonewalling. In the end, the Pargas management paid Empire a substantial premium over the "tender offer" price, a big profit on the Pargas shares Empire owned. Pargas management basically paid Plaster to go away, then continued to own and operate the company as they had before.

Years later the market began to call current management

paying these premiums "green mail" deals, and men like Carl Icahn became wealthy and famous from attempting them. In a textbook green mail deal, the potential buyer buys a large percentage of the stock and then approaches management in hopes that they will pay a big premium to avoid being acquired. Normally the investor has no intention to acquire and operate the company, but only to profit by selling the stock back to current management.

In response, boards of directors began creating "golden parachutes" in their corporate documents to reward current management if an outside party acquired their stock without their consent. "Poison pill" provisions were added for sales not authorized by current management. This penalized an unfriendly buyer, driving up the acquisition costs. Management's jobs were safer, but the shareholders lose when they hold a stock that is inherently more valuable than the current market price.

The important distinction is that Plaster truly wanted to acquire and operate Pargas. Stockholders of both companies would have profited substantially.

Diversification

During the 1970s, Plaster set out to make Empire a totally integrated energy company. Empire Gas Corporation began oil and gas exploration efforts (1973); purchased part of an oil refinery (1976); purchased an underground storage facility in Hutchinson, Kansas (1978); and set up a trading operation in Houston, Texas, to buy and sell petroleum futures (1979), in addition to other petroleum-related investments and related acquisitions.

The numbers-savvy CEO realized rather quickly that the company had no particular expertise in these related fields and that they did not contribute significantly to the bottom line. In fact, the young manager of the petroleum futures trading operation took it upon himself to make several large and speculative "gambles" on the futures market. Plaster discovered the ruse and the horrendous losses incurred but not reported, and shut down the entire operation, but not before Empire had the first negative growth year in the company's history. All outside ventures were divested within a few years.

Plaster instead began to look for contra-seasonal acquisitions. The propane industry makes money typically during the cold five months of the year, and breaks even or loses money in the warmer seven.

A contra-seasonal business would ensure summertime profits so the overall company would be profitable in every quarter. Empire analyzed hundreds of potential acquisitions and tried to acquire at least three companies through tender offers: Biscayne Federal Savings and Loan Association, a Florida-based savings and loan company (1979); Leggett and Platt, Inc., a manufacturer of bed springs and other metal products (1981); and Wetterau, Inc., a wholesale distributor of groceries (1981).

Although Empire sought to own and operate the firms, in each case, management paid Empire a premium for its stock to avoid being taken over. Plaster's wizardry with mathematics and finances made him money but did not fulfill his acquisition goals.

LESSONS LEARNED

1. Follow Up

Plaster kept several secretaries absolutely crazy with his daily, weekly, and monthly lists. His memory was excellent, but he had notes and staff following up on his commitments.

When Bob asked you to do something, he made a note to see if you had done it. When you asked him to do something, he made note of it to be certain that he completed the task you requested. He managed the details of his family and his business in similar fashion, and details made him reliable and brilliant, not to mention respected.

2. Log Calls and Appointments

Bob did not keep a diary, but he kept a private, secured record of calls and appointments. He knew the last time that he talked or met with anyone. With this information available, he could immediately discuss a detail or a deal that he may not have considered in months.

3. Most Jobs Can Be Performed by One Person

Teamwork is emphasized in our schools and business world today, but Bob believed most jobs can be accomplished efficiently and practically by one man or one woman. This belief minimized the daily expenses in his companies and in his life. One person with the responsibility and authority to get the job done means no one shares the praise—or the blame. That is a powerful motivator for a boss who keeps notes on every task and its follow-up.

Bob taught his children not to take on partners, although later in his life Evergreen Investments engaged in projects with some carefully selected partners. All partnerships, like marriages, were negotiated in advance, and every possible eventuality was discussed. The process for dissolution of the partnership was clear in the contracts. Ownership has upsides and downsides, so the percentage of ownership determined the risk and rewards. Thus, he had wonderful partnerships where everyone worked hard, and not incidentally, that makes one lucky.

4. Share the Wealth

Bob had worked in commission sales as a car salesman and in the non-commissioned IRS. He knew incentives worked. Empire Gas Corporation created short-term incentives based on the success of a project or goal and long-term incentive programs based on profits. But because he was frugal and careful with his hard-earned money, the goals were set high—so high that the incentive programs were often met with little enthusiasm from executives or employees. He all too often created a program where no one could win!

So, he decided to share the bottom line. In the last years that he owned Empire Gas Corporation, every operational employee, from the retail management level up, received an annual bonus based on the profitability of his or her respective area of responsibility. When Empire made money, all the appropriate operational management team made money. That strong motivator worked.

5. Bet on Yourself

The world abounds with many types of investments: Some depend on the economy and markets; others depend on the savvy effort of the owners. Bob liked the latter. Betting on yourself is an investment one can manage and control and the result is generally positive for everyone.

CHAPTER 10

CONTROL EXPENSES

Empire Gas Corporation had four management objectives.
1. Make all quotas.
2. Collect accounts receivable.
3. Control expenses.
4. Produce a profit.

Plaster's, and therefore Empire Gas Corporation's, greatest strength was in controlling expenses. The headquarters in Lebanon, Missouri, was cheaper to operate than it would have been in a large city, although a city might have provided beneficial relationships.

Robert W. Plaster, Chairman and CEO, Empire Incorporated, *Financial World* **magazine, February 15, 1981**

Two or three levels of management approved, or renegotiated, every expenditure as Empire stayed solvent and profitable through good times and hard. Plaster would remind his employees and his family, "If you take care of the pennies, the dollars will take care of themselves." He meant it, and he instituted controls even as his company spent millions of dollars a year. A penny per dollar sales, or a penny per hour man-power purchased, or a penny per employee benefit, could amount to hundreds, thousands, or millions of dollars. He watched pennies.

Bob would also say that it was much easier to SAVE a dollar, than it was to MAKE a dollar. A dollar of sales revenue contributes but a small "margin" to the bottom line. Reducing a dollar of cost instantly increases the bottom line by the full dollar.

In later years, Bob would say that the only thing he could not give his children was the knowledge of what it was like to be poor. Like so many Depression babies, he was frugal with how he spent his money, the company's money, the family's money, and his investor's money. His philosophy was:

1. Never spend a dollar until you absolutely have to.
2. Never buy more than you need.
3. When you need it, buy it at the lowest possible price.

Dad gave his children an allowance to spend as we pleased—after the half that went to our bank account as savings. My first weekly allowance was a nickel in the early 1960s. My first job, mucking horse stalls on the ranch, paid two dollars an hour, with half to my savings account. My siblings and I balanced our checkbooks and calculated our interest monthly. Dad believed in saving money and made sure each of his children understood the importance.

Today there are 401(k)s, certificates of deposit, various stock market products, REITs (real estate investment trusts), and a multitude of ways to save. Then there were only savings accounts.

The point is to save, so you have money for a bargain that comes along, or if something goes wrong you are not forced to borrow or sell assets in a hurry.. Financial stability means having enough money in reserve to manage the unforeseen, and it helps you sleep at night. Studies even tell us that people with financial stability live healthier and longer.

Some people seem to believe that as long as they have checks or credit they have money. Knowing how much money you have sets the stage for spending only what you can afford. It is easy to have the electric company auto-debit your account and the utility loves it—because now they have control of your money. But only you should be responsible for your money, and no one else should ever have that control. If you are willing to give someone else control of your money, then you are willing to give them your money.

—*Stephen*

Bob would say money was not the ultimate measure of success, "but it's a great way to keep score." No one had the authority to debit or remove money from Bob's personal or his firm's accounts. Ever.

Facing Detractors

No successful business grows without detractors, and the firm hand Bob maintained with his businesses saved him more than once. In 1972, Empire Gas was charged with "aiding and abetting in the illegal possession of an unregistered firearm," which resulted in a four-and-a-half-year investigation. Anti-trust charges were brought and thoroughly investigated.

Bob's control over his company meant he knew what the company did and did not do, and he was able to defend himself. At the trial, the judge expressed his resentment against the government attorneys for the waste of taxpayer money, exonerated Empire with a total acquittal, and assessed the costs of both trials to the government.

CHAPTER 11

POLITICS

Bob Plaster viewed politics, politicians, and the political climate as vitally important to any business. His frugality did not allow him to be as open-handed as he might have liked, but he enjoyed friendships with many highly-praised politicians and always cultivated and enjoyed knowing the incumbent Governor of the State of Missouri.

Plaster was a Christian first, an American second, a conservative third, and a Republican somewhere further down that line. It was not uncommon for him to support a very conservative Democrat rather than the opposing less conservative Republican. Plaster was not the kind of fellow to boast about his politics, his pride in America, or his conservative nature. Instead, he made it obvious in the way he lived his life. He did not preach. He did not rant about his beliefs. But he would give you his opinion if you asked.

As the years went by, he became more and more involved in politics, not by spending enormous sums of money as some corporations do, but by befriending politicians. Many politicians became his good friends and friends of the family. He did

President George W. Bush landing on a re-election campaign stop in Missouri, 2004

Above: The Plaster children in politics, left to right, Cheryl Wrinkle, daughter; Governor Mitt Romney, Republican Presidential Nominee; Robert W. Plaster; Tammy Brown, daughter; Stephen Plaster, son; Matt Blunt, Governor of Missouri; Larry Weis, Evergreen Investment's Chief Financial Officer, 2008

Left: Robert Plaster and Oliver North at funraiser, circa 2005

Bob Plaster and the Go:vernor of Arkansas, later Presidential candidate and successful media personality, Mike Huckabee, hunting ducks in Arkansas, circa 2006

Dressed for the Governor's Ball circa 1965

support them, but he did so judiciously. He also shared with them hunting opportunities on the ranch and often sponsored fundraisers at the company's classic car facility to assist them in gaining more supporters. Later in life he delighted in the engaging company of the Speaker of the U.S. House of Representatives Newt Gingrich of Georgia and served on his ten-man advisory board. Senator Kit Bond, Senator John Ashcroft (who later became Attorney General of the United States), Congressional leader Roy Blunt, Governor of Missouri Matt Blunt, and a host of others were welcome guests.

The expression of your right to petition is so important that it is a big part of the First Amendment in the Bill of Rights. Most politicians are sincere, well-meaning Americans who seize the opportunity to be informed and to do the right thing. Plaster never ignored this side of business and he worked with, supported, talked to, and got to know politicians so that when he had an opinion, he could encourage them to make informed decisions.

America fought a war with the English king because he would not listen to the Colonists. Businessmen have the right and duty to help their government run well. Many people become conditioned to believe that their vote doesn't count, is not important, and will not change anything. Plaster never missed an opportunity to vote and taught his children and executives that it was one of the most important things that an American can do to improve their world.

> *During college I mentioned to Dad that I was considering a career in politics. Dad's tongue-in-cheek response was, "You're a lot better off to own one than to be one." Dad made it clear that he did not mean to buy politicians. An individual can, however, influence who wins an election by working with and donating to candidates who hold views that you agree with.*
>
> *Knowing the levels of government and knowing elected officials as people, educating and explaining your views to them after they trust you, and adding your expertise to policy discussions is what I knew Dad wanted me to do.* —Stephen

CHAPTER 12

EMPIRE AND "PRIVATE" OWNERSHIP

Working on financial deals, tender offers, and other investments opportunities introduced Plaster to New York City and a multitude of financial players always open to new opportunities. In late 1982, Plaster was approached by a group of private investors led by Allen & Company of New York who wanted to acquire all of the outstanding stock of Empire Gas Corporation and make it a privately owned company again. Leveraged buyouts were the latest investment trend, and banks were willing to finance, in many cases, 100 percent of the purchase price.

Empire Gas Corporation ceased to exist as a publicly traded entity, but the private company was highly leveraged. "Servicing the debt," which means paying the interest and principal on the loan, required every dollar of the working capital.

The Federal Reserve, a private bank set up in the 1930s, manages the U.S. money supply with two goals: achieving maximum sustainable employment and maintaining a stable inflation rate. The two goals can be in conflict with each other. During the oil and energy crises of the President Carter years in the 1970s, the U.S. endured "stagflation," a stagnant economy and high inflation. The prime lending rate, which had been 10 percent to 12 percent, skyrocketed to more than 20 percent. The new Empire Gas Corporation's variable interest rate loans were tied to the prime lending rate, so the cost of its debt was now more than 26 percent per year. Empire Gas Corporation adapted, changed the way it did business, drastically cut expenses, and weathered the storm.

When President Ronald Reagan was elected in 1980, the independent Federal Reserve changed policy to put inflation control as its highest policy priority.

The overall economy improved and interest rates declined. In a few short years, the owners, led by Allen & Company and others, approached Plaster about selling. With funds from his tender offers and the equity of his executives, Plaster negotiated better financing from a few banks and acquired Empire again. Interest rates were still record-high and only good, tight, conservative management kept the company in business and growing.

Empire Divides

In 1994, Plaster was approached by one of his most trusted executives, then Empire's Vice Chairman, who had wanted to run his own propane gas company for many years. Roughly half of the management team put up the equity and bought roughly half of Empire Gas Corporation. The acquiring entity kept the Empire Gas Corporation name, most of the debt, half the management team, and leased half the home office building.

The Plaster family continued to operate the other half of the company under the name Evergreen Energy. Bob's son Stephen had been the President of Empire Gas and became President and Chief Operating Officer of Evergreen Energy.

Plaster's age, and his estate planning attorneys, encouraged him to "get some more eggs out of that basket." In 1997, the remainder of the company was sold to a South Dakota public utility.

The original Empire was sold in two pieces. Both were taken over by managers with entirely different operating styles and within five years both were bankrupt.

> *Employees retired over the years, but a lot of employees remained with the company through thick and thin. After the final Empire sale, only a few employees remained as Bob left propane management and shifted to private equity investments through his new company structure, Evergreen Investments, LLC.*
>
> *Bob's trusted Administrative Assistant, Carolyn Rein, single-handedly managed all the dictation, filing, follow-up notes, and nitpicking details that helped the company thrive. Carolyn made Bob's job easier every minute of every day.*
>
> *Earl Noe as Vice President oversaw insurance, litigation, and a variety of challenging executive assignments. He said what he thought was right even when it wasn't popular and remained our gyroscope.*
>
> *A great supporter and trusted confidant, Larry Weis, who had started in our Audit Department in 1984, remained as Chief Financial Officer (CFO). Larry is my "adopted brother," smarter than I am, with the best historical memory of anyone I have ever known. In many respects, Dad treated him better than he did me! Empire employees worked hard, and Dad and I appreciated them and their lives, well-being, and families. With Evergreen, we were a small, lean company again. —Stephen*

CHAPTER 13

EVERGREEN INVESTMENTS

Not thinking about propane distribution was a big change. The national economy was strong when the remaining part of Empire Gas Corporation was sold. Plaster had an enviable cash position but acquisition candidates were hard to come by at reasonable prices. Plaster and his small team looked hard for a suitable business segment to enter through acquisition or start-up.

Bob and Stephen Plaster followed the principle "make your money on the buy side" in their propane acquisitions, and knew that every business or venture translates a physical product or a service into revenue. Paying more for a product or labor decreases the margin unless prices increase. Price increases run the risk of losing customers. Wise purchases automatically increase the margins at any revenue level.

Many people (especially politicians) think it should be easy to pay a little bit more here and there, then make it up in sales and revenues. As a practical matter, controlling costs on the buy side so that prices do not increase is essential for any investment deal to work.

Bob's Exception

After the recession of 1982, a booming economy and the country and western-themed tourism in nearby Branson, Missouri, changed the rustic nature of the family's peaceful Lake of the Ozarks vacations. The lake house had been a respite from the Empire Ranch, and it was a place for family and business guests to enjoy.

Evergreen Investments Executive Headquarters on Table Rock Lake near Branson, Missouri

Lake pollution was the final straw and Plaster decided to sell and move the family to Table Rock Lake. The lake house he started building got bigger, better, and more expensive—too fancy and expensive to risk letting the kids and pets enjoy. The 24,000-square-foot facility dubbed "Evergreen" cost millions of dollars to build and held furniture and furnishings from all over the world. It contained a dozen state-of-the-art guest suites, a helicopter landing pad, an indoor shooting range, and a twelve-car garage. All were designed with grand views of Table Rock Lake.

When Stephen questioned the surprising Table Rock Lake extravagances in blatant contradiction to his father's frugal nature, Bob recalled the time an East Coast stockbroker had flown to Lebanon, Missouri. When he stepped off the plane, the stockbroker looked at Bob and Steve in business suits and exclaimed, "Gee, being in Missouri I expected to see you guys barefooted and in bib overalls." They laughed and conducted their business. Bob never mentioned how much the incident bothered him.

When questioned by his son about the high construction costs, he recalled the bib overall comment and told his son, "I remember a time when all I could afford was bare feet and bib overalls. I want to build a place we can bring executives from anywhere in the world and they will be suitably impressed."

The facility became the executive headquarters and hosted business meetings, closings, fundraisers, and many successful negotiations. In his will, Bob donated the Evergreen facility to the Robert W. Plaster Foundation so that it, or funds from its sale, would continue to be used for philanthropic and educational endeavors.

Champion Brands

The first acquisition completed after the last Empire sale was the Lowe Oil Company in Clinton, Missouri. The Lowe family had built the company into a nice regional blender and bottler of automotive chemicals. They owned the "Champion" trademark for anything automotive, excluding spark plugs.

The youngest of the three Lowe brothers, David, decided to reinvest in the company under the new ownership. David took the reins as President of that company and has grown, doubled, and redoubled the new Champion Brands. David's greatest strengths are very similar to Bob Plaster's. Singleness of purpose, expense control, Christian faith, and a rock-solid work ethic have helped push Champion to a commanding position in that industry.

Researching New Businesses

Evergreen sold a wonderful piece of real estate to Walmart and kept the best out-lot, the small part of a big parcel of land that is on the outside, usually on the street. There Evergreen created five start-up businesses: a car wash, a convenience store, a frozen custard drive-in, a laundromat, and a liquor store. The goal was to find solid businesses, build more, create a chain, develop economies of scale, and enjoy the synergies. In the final analysis, none of the businesses warranted expansion or even continued investment. The businesses were sold.

One day, Bob and Stephen began talking about a deal Evergreen turned down that turned out to be very successful for the new owners. Then they talked about a few other deals they did that made money for their investors. Bob looked at Stephen and said, "More importantly, there have been very few deals we did and should not have done."

EVERGREEN INVESTMENTS

Fountain at Branson Landing, circa 2008

Dad knew enough about every job in our company to know how to do it, and his people knew it. His employees also realized they would be out of a job if he was the one who had to do it!

One time our convenience store floor was proving to be a maintenance nightmare. Although the tile was mopped daily, it never looked clean. Dad complained, and finally one day asked for a scrub brush, a bucket, Spic and Span®, and warm water. He showed up at the convenience store, gathered the team, and scrubbed one area to a lustrous white shine. Then he changed to clean rinse water and rinsed. For a day or two that was the only white spot on the floor in the whole store. After that the whole floor suddenly became white as the employees realized that if the boss could do it, it could be done, and they had better get it done. —Stephen

Real Estate Development

Contrary to Plaster's philosophy of never doing business with a partner, he began a series of real estate developments with three partners, Rick Huffman, Sam Catanese, and Mark Williams, and their development company known as HCW Development. The first development, Branson Landing in Branson, Missouri, included two Hilton Hotels, 440,000 square feet of retail space, and hundreds of condominiums.

Huffman is a magical negotiator and has since led the partnership to include retail centers, apartments, condominiums, and other profitable real estate ventures.

Business Cycles

Another way to lose money is to get in a position where one has to sell in a down market. The economy is a web of industries that ebb and flow in different cycles. Evergreen receives offers to invest in things "that can never lose money." Classic cars, firearms, gold and jewelry, and real estate may be more stable than other investments, but they are not producing dividends and are affected by inflation and markets. To be solid investments, the investor must be able to hold these asset classes through downturns.

Real estate is expensive and generally goes up in value, but values can collapse in a city, state, or the entire country as it did during the financial banking collapse of 2008. These are circumstances beyond your control. Over-building or a new tax can crush the values, a factory shuts its doors, or a highway changes the traffic patterns. The landlord still pays insurance, interest and principle, overhead, property taxes, repairs, and a lot of other expenses. With planning and a sufficient budget or savings, the odds are good that the investment will begin producing positive cash flow before the funding runs out in the long term. If one has to sell when the market is down in order to pay debt, property tax, maintenance, insurance, or tide over a vacancy, the investor can lose all gains. Hard asset investments require a strategy that allows for market swings.

Evergreen Investments plans its capital requirements and how additional funds will be added if necessary. Harkening back to the days when Bob Plaster calculated the contingency plans in his head, he taught his financial team to plan for contingencies and to avoid the deals that sound too good to be true. Assumptions or calculations that do not match the most likely real-world scenario are figured and refigured.

Nevertheless, some deals do not work as intended, and then additional funds are required. Some deals will never work, even throwing good money after bad—Evergreen calls these "deals with a sucking sound." Programming your investments with a downside cap helps you know and avoid the risk that everyone feels about a deal gone sour.

LESSONS LEARNED

1. Own the Surrounding Land

A salvage yard or other eyesore built in front of even the most magnificent house or beautiful commercial office can wipe out the value. Plaster controlled his own destiny by owning as much land as possible around any real estate or building project. This simple investment strategy pays many dividends and is a source of pride for everyone in the company.

2. Return OF Investment

One bad deal can wipe out the positives created by several good deals. Return OF investment is often more important than return ON investment. When textbooks talk about "preservation of capital," the phrase means guarding your nest egg—that dollar-by-dollar fund earned and saved to invest.

Executives, investment advisors, stockbrokers, and other money managers talk about rates of return. Too often they refer to "relative" rates of return rather than true rates of return. Five percent better than the Dow Jones Industrial Average might sounds good at first blush, but if the market went down 50 percent and your investment fund only went down 45 percent, the REAL rate of return was negative 45 percent.

Only when the investor takes into consideration the cash cycles, the upside and the downside, tax implications, and a host of other risk-reward considerations and alternative scenarios will he/she be prepared to know what is and is not a good investment. After the Depression and before the age of the 401(k) in the 1980s, a worker may have had a defined benefit pension plan in retirement. Then, businesses took on the risks of pension investments. Today, workers are more likely to have to know what to expect with what they put away for investment and for retirement. The world of the relative rate of return is worth understanding.

Politicians talk about cutting a budget, but they usually only mean cutting the rate of increase in the budget. When a household has to tighten its belt, it is actually spending less. The government seldom spends less on anything; it cuts the rate of increase in spending. Know your math and the terms of the industry before you decide to save, spend, or vote.

> *For several decades, Dad and I served on the board of a small rural college with Christian roots and a substantial endowment. The stock market was strong and the investment committee, guided by outside money managers, kept increasing the percentage of the endowment in the stock market. Plasters are wary of the stock market; Dad felt it was artificially high and driven by speculation, and he warned that preservation of capital was essential. He recommended interest-bearing securities that guaranteed a return of capital and paid a predetermined interest rate.*
>
> *The investment committee decided instead to put more funds into the equity market because the continued escalation of values looked like it would never stop. When the stock market corrected, half the endowment fund was wiped out. The college survived, but had to re-build the endowment.*
>
> *Not all deals are worth investing in for every entity, even if they make some people money. There are two important components to any investment decision and they are knowing when to get IN and knowing when to get OUT.* —Stephen

3. Use Firm but Fair Management

Bob Plaster used a firm but fair management style. When circumstances dictated away from normal, he let employees know the bosses were making an exception. Fair works out—punitive or ruthless rarely does. Not surprisingly, when the last portion of Empire was sold, Plaster kept a handful of dedicated employees who had worked together for decades. Organizational duties were divided up and everyone worked hard operating current businesses, adding new acquisitions, and reinvesting funds. When circumstances dictate away from normal, let people know that you are making an exception.

Plaster was always tough or "firm" in business. Everyone around him knew it and it became his trademark. He remained very fair when it came to exercising the authority that only he had. This made it easy to earn and keep loyalty from his employees and respect from employees and competitors.

CHAPTER 14

THE FOUNDATION AND PHILANTHROPY

Early in his business career, Plaster endowed anonymous scholarships with a variety of colleges. The individual recipients and the Plaster family were not privy to the scholarship details. The exception was the scholarship he created in his mother's name to a college in Neosho, Missouri.

Later, Plaster changed his philosophy to help the many rather than the few. He chose to donate toward buildings on college campuses, called "naming gifts," because they are large donations that allow the donor to name the building. Plaster came to believe that helping a school build a building would lower the cost of education for all its students, and hopefully provide an example of giving back for all to see and follow.

Lebanon Daily Record, **January 9, 1980**

Robert W. Plaster Free Enterprise Center at Missouri Southern State University, Joplin, Missouri, Bob's alma mater

Robert W. Plaster Free Enterprise Center, Okark Technical College, Table Rock Campus, Hollister, Missouri

Robert W. Plaster Business Incubator at Missouri State University, Springfield, Missouri

Robert W. Plaster Free Enterprise Center, Students in Free Enterprise (SIFE) headquarters, Springfield, Missouri

In the early 1980s, Plaster created the perpetual Robert W. Plaster Foundation with brilliant attorneys and aspiring executives. The Plaster Family's contributions are invested carefully with the intention to continue providing naming gifts for bricks and mortar projects long into the future.

Students in Free Enterprise

Plaster believed in the free enterprise system because it was in no small part responsible for his success. His commitment to the nonprofit Students in Free Enterprise (SIFE) is part of his legacy.

SIFE was founded by businessmen in Texas to teach the gospel of the free enterprise system. The new President Alvin Rohrs was fresh out of law school when his first major decision was to move the organization to his hometown of Bolivar, Missouri. SIFE had a handful of member schools, and Rohrs approached Dr. Jim Sells, President of Southwest Baptist College, about hosting the new organization. President Sells told Plaster, "I have an organization here that you will be very interested in." Plaster met with Rohrs and then called Sam Walton, founder of Walmart, and said, "I have an organization here that you will be very interested in." Walton sent a young executive from Walmart, Jack Shewmaker, to mentor SIFE.

SIFE grew exponentially and involved hundreds of CEOs, presidents, and business owners from every walk of life during the next thirty years. Plaster recruited many great friends and met many new ones as they encouraged hundreds of thousands of college students to learn and then spread the gospel of the free enterprise system, to teach it to the world, and to use it to help the world.

Alvin Rohrs grew in his position as a result of his hard work and mentoring from Bob Plaster, Jack Shewmaker, and others. He became as close to Bob Plaster as any son. After Plaster passed in 2008, the name of the organization was changed, their mission statement drifted, the goals changed, and it became unrecognizable as the champion of free enterprise. Rohrs retired in 2016.

CHAPTER 15

FAMILY

Plaster worked hard from childhood to the age of seventy-eight, and he expected his family to work as hard with the same Can't Never Could philosophy as their guide. His son Stephen would joke that Bob Plaster "had cut back to half days" because twelve hours of the twenty-four-hour day was all the family could get him to work.

Plaster spent a lot of time creating and planning his estate.

Plaster family at Dolly's Wedding, 1996

Plaster family at Bob and Jean's fiftieth Wedding Anniversary, 2001

Plaster family at Tammy's wedding, 1996

The four Plaster boys: Robert Wayne, son Stephen Robert, grandson Michael Robert, and cousin Thomas Harold, circa 2007

His biggest fear was that leaving money to his family would create "a bunch of trust fund brats that do nothing but live off the inheritance." The following paragraph is from one of the Plaster trusts:

"In creating separate trust estates for his children, grandchildren, and more remote biological descendants (each of whom is herein referred to as a "Descendant Beneficiary"), it is Grantor's intent to encourage exceptional character and behavior in the Descendant Beneficiaries. Specifically, it is Grantor's intent to encourage the Descendant Beneficiaries to pursue the finest education their abilities allow, to work hard, to be gainfully employed and economically self-sustaining, to marry, to raise children (if possible), and to give back to their communities. It is Grantor's intent to encourage such character and behavior without creating a class of Descendant Beneficiaries who accomplish nothing in life other than collecting benefits from the trust estates held hereunder. In this connection, Grantor has crafted the provisions of this Agreement governing these trust estates to encourage the Descendant Beneficiaries to develop a work ethic that will make them productive in life" —Robert Plaster Trust

So, his trusts have strict rules. Work is essential, and, if the rules are followed, the beneficiaries might receive remuneration. If the rules are not followed, even a family member receives nothing. The foundation receives any planned distribution if the family member does not qualify.

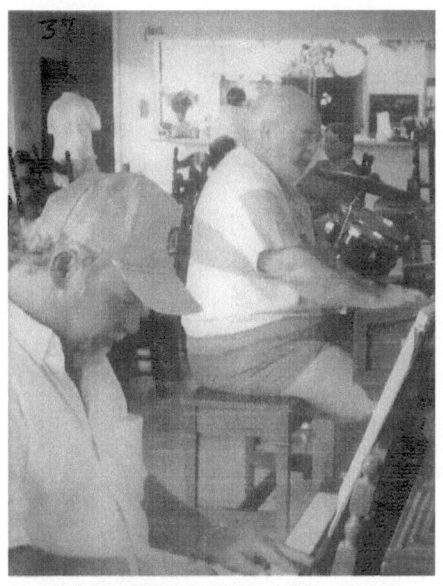

Stephen (foreground) and Bob jam together, circa 2006

Music

Bob lived a balanced life and his family reflects the care he took. He kept many musical instruments at his house that no one could play. When a visitor said, "Gee, if you had a clarinet, I'd play, too," he produced one. Amazing, impromptu jam sessions resulted in the liberating musical atmosphere.

And, of course, there were many times the family would gather around the piano and sing. Not that the Plasters enjoy perfect pitch or even fine resonance; some may say they cannot sing well. But no one can say it isn't fun and enjoyable with lots of laughs!

Fun and Games

In the early 1970's, Plaster was persuaded to invest in horses as a profit center for the ranch. He jumped into registered thoroughbred breeding in a big way. At our highest point, he had 99 registered thoroughbred horses and 49 registered quarter horses. The ranch also had four barns with almost 100 stalls, maternity and breeding stalls, and a 7/8ths mile practice race track.

Bob said he lost enough money on horses to retire. One of Stephen's first official jobs was cleaning stalls for the ranch's herd of horses. As a consequence of both, the Plasters never owned horses again, except as a hobby. They switched horse powers.

Above: Bob and his favorite car, a 1931 Chrysler model CG Imperial dual cowl phaeton, circa 2008.

Left: Bob at one of many antique car auctions, circa 2007

CHAPTER 16

EVERGREEN HISTORIC AUTOMOBILES

Like so many young men, Bob Plaster wanted a car before he could afford one. Then he wanted a newer or better car. Long before he could afford the car he wanted, he was fanatical about the appearance and maintenance of the ones he did have.

When he began to acquire a little disposable income, Bob found that playing with antique cars was fun. He started purchasing a few old cars for the family to fix and enjoy.

In 1978, the major American automobile companies announced that they were downsizing the American automobile to comply with the government's fuel/mileage mandates. Plaster was absolutely spastic, "I will never drive a small car."

A few weeks later, Plaster announced that he had ordered two new Cadillacs and two new Lincolns to last the rest of his life, and that he would NEVER have to drive a small car. The next question was, where to keep four new cars? The family brainstormed and decided to disassemble a metal hay barn from the ranch, move it up the hill behind the main Plaster house, reassemble it, and create "The Car Barn."

Speaker Dennis Hastert and Bob Plaster enjoyed cars together, circa 2005

The Car Barn's extra space allowed room for additional cars. A 1951 Pontiac coupe, a 1931 Ford sedan, and a 1951 Chevrolet coupe were first, and before long the whole building was full of old cars, most in stages of imperfect but drivable condition.

Plaster quickly learned that the right automobile, maintained in an exceptional fashion, was a good investment. He sold every car except the convertibles, low production models, and cars of substantial historical significance because they increase in value faster than their hardtop counterparts. From that point forward, the antique cars were treated as a long-term investment much like fine art would be—but more fun. Cars were added, cars were sold, cars were always maintained and always cherished.

So many visitors came to the Car Barn that a small dining room was created within the collection that drew parties, receptions, successful business meetings, and endless reminiscences and conversation. Plaster's car inventory totaled more than 300 automobiles, virtually all convertibles, and represented 78 dif-

I had been pestering Dad to attend one of the big car auctions in Scottsdale, Arizona. He said he didn't have time. One day he called from Washington, D.C. He had just met the new Speaker of the United States House of Representatives, Dennis Hastert of Illinois.

"Do you still want to go to that auction?"

"Well of course!"

"Well, I'll pick you up in two hours."

The Speaker was a "car guy" who also wanted to see the Scottsdale car auction and who kept a packed schedule. This was before the days of regulations that precluded such an adventure for an elected official. Dad said, "My plane's here and let's go."

They stopped in Lebanon, Missouri, for me; then we spent the night in Scottsdale, went to the auctions, and came back to Lebanon the next day.

The Speaker visited several times over the next few years, and I would spend the day driving cars out of the building while Dad and the Speaker drove them around the ranch. Every fifteen or twenty minutes they would park one car and jump in the one I had just started. Those were great days! —Stephen

ferent automobile manufacturers before he left this earth. The legacy continues.

Today, Lebanon, Missouri's Evergreen Historic Automobiles (www.evergreenhistoricautomobiles.com) is one of the largest and most respected assemblages of automobiles in the world, with nearly 500 unusual or rare cars, 150,000 square feet, and a charity and fundraiser banquet area of more than 5,000 square feet. Tours are booked by appointment only months in advance. Although the cars are bought, sold, and managed as investments, Plaster was quick to point out that they are non-cash-flow-producing investments

Evergreen Historic Automobiles employs a team of experts to repair, restore, and maintain the automobile portfolio. Several of the staff have a bachelor's degree in Automobile Restoration from McPherson College in McPherson, Kansas. Involving these young people has the added benefit of encouraging the next generation of automobile enthusiasts and investors.

CHAPTER 17

HEALTH

Robert Plaster was 6' 4" and 350–400 pounds most of his life. He remained incredibly healthy, perhaps because he concentrated so much energy on fueling his systems well. He took a great interest in his health, studied, and learned. If he read about a vitamin that did something he thought he needed, he started taking it.

Bob Plaster was always very health conscious and encouraged the same in his employees.

Plaster recognized that health in his executives was vitally important. An innovation at the time, health insurance was available through the company, and top management received an annual doctor's physical at company expense. Executives were expected to go. Plaster encouraged his executives, family, and friends to exercise, eat right, and to take appropriate vitamins.

Empire Gas Corporation was one of the first nationwide companies to build an executive athletic facility at their headquarters. Unusual and even extravagant for the time, the building was heated and air conditioned so it was comfortable year-round and included full-sized basketball, handball, and indoor tennis courts and weight training facilities. Bob would joke that the employee athletic facility was Evergreen's "most under-deployed asset."

> *The vitamins worked. Eight years before Dad died, a doctor in Springfield, Missouri, insisted he needed open heart surgery today or he would not live to see tomorrow. Doctors who examined him before and during those eight years commented that his blood flow and pressure, chemistry, and vital statistics were that of a much younger man. He and I attributed that to his insistence that his body get the fuel it needed through vitamins and health food. Still, he was reluctant to have the open heart surgery. On October 11, 2008, Dad worked 12 hours, drove 100 miles to spend the night with his family, and died peacefully in his sleep. —Stephen*

LESSONS LEARNED

1. Keep Learning

Although Plaster could not afford to finish college, he was extremely smart and well-read, with the additional asset of having a lifetime of common sense drilled into him. He worked at staying ahead of everyone else. He subscribed to and read some fifty periodicals cover to cover. He watched the news and made it a point to stay abreast of worldwide current events. As a consequence, his conversations were wide-ranging, informed, and interesting.

He subscribed to the adage "knowledge is power" and encouraged his executives and family to follow his lead. To thrive in the real world, one needs to know how to connect to people, events, and thus to trends and investments.

2. Earn Your Luck

Bob believed the harder he worked the luckier he got. Successful people did not get to success based on luck, they worked hard and poured blood, sweat, and tears into their endeavors. From the outside looking in they appear to have been lucky.

Robert W. and Stephen Plaster, circa 2005

AFTERWORD

I watched Bob Plaster lead by example for fifty years. Looking back on this book I realize I have probably given you the impression that I thought he was perfect. He was not perfect. Like the rest of us, he was human. He was forthright. He was honest. He was ambitious. And he was opinionated. He was stubborn. He was patriotic. He was humble. He was competitive. And he was driven. His greatest strength was probably his willingness to learn. Many people claim to have a desire to learn, but they get so smart, or so powerful, that they become obsessed with trying to show everyone how smart or important they are. Bob Plaster was not that guy.

Bob Plaster was that rare, gentle giant who would ask questions and then shut up and truly listen to the answers. By listening, he learned. He was also that guy who would ask you a question that he already knew the answer to. (In fact, I learned early on that he rarely ever asked a question he did not already know the answer to!) He was that guy who made others think and learn as well. He was that guy who would let you make mistakes so you could learn from them. And he was that guy who would keep you from making mistakes he thought might get you hurt.

His secret to success? Hard work. He wasted no time, energy, or money on anything that did not improve his business, his family, his Net worth, or his friends, at any time.

What he did was something that anyone could do. He worked hard. He worked hard to the exclusion of many other fun things. And I will be the first to concede that he often found a way to engineer fun things so that he could further his business objectives while having fun. A couple of examples might be the networking done at Empire Ranch or activities associated with the classic car investments. He was the best friend, or the worst enemy, that anyone could have, depending on which would help you the most. He was a great mentor. He was a great teacher. And he was a great father.

—Stephen R. Plaster

APPENDIX

PROFESSIONAL BIO

Robert W. Plaster
Palm Beach, Florida
December 2007

CORPORATE POSITIONS
Chairman of the Board, Champion Brands
Chairman of the Board and President, Empire Pipeline Corporation
Chairman of the Board, Empire Ranch, Inc.
Chairman of the Board, Evergreen Investments, LLC
Chairman of the Board and President, Evergreen National Corporation
Chairman of the Board, Evergreen Exploration

PHILANTHROPY (partial listing)
Elsie Plaster Community Center, Crowder College
Robert W. Plaster Athletic Center, Robert W. Plaster Business Dormitory, Robert W. Plaster Stadium, Southwest Baptist University
Robert W. Plaster Free Enterprise Center and the Campus, Students in Free Enterprise
Funded Robert W. Plaster School of Business Administration and Robert W. Plaster Free Enterprise Center, Missouri Southern State University
Robert W. Plaster School of Business Building, Elmer Braswell Building, The College of the Ozarks
Robert W. Plaster Sports Complex and the Robert W. Plaster Student Union, Missouri State University

SERVICE

32nd Degree Mason, Laclede Lodge Number 33
Abou Ben Adem Shrine, Springfield, Missouri
Board of Directors, UMB Financial Corporation
Board of Directors and Executive Committee, Students in Free Enterprise
Board of Trustees, The College of the Ozarks, 1978-2003
Member, Beta Gamma Sigma
Member, First United Methodist Church, Lebanon, Missouri
Hickory Hills Country Club, Springfield, Missouri
Kansas City Club, Kansas City, Missouri
Shriner, Scottish Rite of Freemasonry and York Rite
Turnberry Yacht & Racquet Club, Miami, Florida

VOLUNTEERISM

Board of Trustees, Southwest Baptist University Foundation, Bolivar, Missouri
Director, National LP Gas Association
Director, Sharon Steel Corporation
Officer, Missouri National Guard
President, Kiwanis Club, Lebanon, Missouri
President, Missouri State University Foundation, Springfield, Missouri

EDUCATION

Attended Missouri Southern State University
Doctor of Business Administration, Southwest Baptist University (Honorary)
Doctor of Humane Letters, Missouri Southern State University (Honorary)

NOTES

www.ingramcontent.com/pod-product-compliance
Lightning Source LLC
Chambersburg PA
CBHW020432220526
45464CB00002B/666